The Monroe Doctrine
The Birth of American Foreign Policy

Robert M. Hamilton

PowerKids
press™

NEW YORK

Published in 2017 by The Rosen Publishing Group, Inc.
29 East 21st Street, New York, NY 10010

Book Design: Samantha DeMartin
Editor: Katie Kawa

Photo Credits: Cover https://commons.wikimedia.org/wiki/File:James_Monroe_Cabinet.jpg; p. 4 https://commons.wikimedia.org/wiki/File:James_Monroe_White_House_portrait_1819.gif; p. 5 courtesy of the National Archives; p. 6 https://commons.wikimedia.org/wiki/File:John_Quincy_Adams_by_GPA_Healy,_1858.jpg; p. 7 Tetra Images/Getty Images; pp. 8, 21 MPI/Archive Photos/Getty Images; p. 9 Three Lions/Hulton Archive/Getty Images; p. 10 DEA/M. SEEMULLER/De Agostini Picture Library/Getty Images; p. 11 https://commons.wikimedia.org/wiki/File:Austerlitz-baron-Pascal.jpg; p. 12 Print Collector/Hulton Archive/Getty Images; p. 13 https://commons.wikimedia.org/wiki/File:Flickr_-_USCapitol_-_The_Monroe_Doctrine,_1823.jpg; p. 15 Everett Historical/Shutterstock.com; p. 16 Buyenlarge/Archive Photos/Getty Images; p. 17 Fotosearch/Archive Photos/Getty Images; p. 19 DEA PICTURE LIBRARY/De Agostini/Getty Images; p. 20 SuperStock/Getty Images.

Cataloging-in-Publication Data

Names: Hamilton, Robert M.
Title: The Monroe Doctrine: the birth of American foreign policy / Robert M. Hamilton.
Description: New York : PowerKids Press, 2016. | Series: Spotlight on American history | Includes index.
Identifiers: ISBN 9781508149590 (pbk.) | ISBN 9781508149248 (6 pack) | ISBN 9781508149453 (library bound)
Subjects: LCSH: Monroe doctrine--Juvenile literature. | United States--Foreign relations--Europe--Juvenile literature. | Europe--Foreign relations--United States--Juvenile literature.
Classification: LCC JZ1482.H36 2016 | DDC 327.7304--dc23

Manufactured in the United States of America

CPSIA Compliance Information: Batch #BS16PK: For further information contact Rosen Publishing, New York, New York at 1-800-237-9932.

CONTENTS

FOREIGN POLICY FOUNDATIONS

Today, the United States is known as a world power, and its influence is felt around the globe. However, this wasn't always the case. For nearly 50 years after the United States gained its independence from Britain, it didn't have a clear foreign policy, or approach for dealing with other countries. However, as the United States grew in size and strength, it was clear the groundwork needed to be laid for a **uniquely** American foreign policy.

That groundwork came in the form of the Monroe Doctrine of 1823. This doctrine, or official statement of government policy,

James Monroe

The Monroe Doctrine, shown here, wasn't known by that name at first. In fact, it took decades before people began referring to this foreign policy statement as the "Monroe Doctrine."

was delivered by President James Monroe in his yearly address to Congress. Although the Monroe Doctrine didn't immediately change the way other countries saw the United States, it became the foundation on which U.S. foreign policy was built. It also hinted at the influence the United States would have beyond its own expanding borders.

ROOTS OF THE MONROE DOCTRINE

The points stated in the Monroe Doctrine were rooted in beliefs as old as the nation itself. The Monroe Doctrine stated that the Western Hemisphere was closed to further colonization. The United States itself was once a group of European colonies that fought for freedom. It made sense that its leaders would want to fight against colonization and support independent nations in the Western Hemisphere.

John Quincy Adams

George Washington believed the United States should stay out of European affairs. This was an important part of his farewell address, and it also became an important part of the Monroe Doctrine.

However, the Monroe Doctrine also stated that the United States wouldn't interfere with colonies that already existed in the Western Hemisphere. Monroe said the United States would stay out of conflicts between European countries, too. This was something President George Washington encouraged in his 1796 farewell address. Washington warned against becoming tangled up in the problems of European nations. Monroe and his **secretary of state**, John Quincy Adams, seemed to share these concerns.

RUSSIA'S INFLUENCE

During the early 1800s, many nations were trying to gain control of parts of the Western Hemisphere. One of these nations was Russia. While it's well known that Russia controlled land in what's now Alaska, it's not as well known that it also controlled land in present-day California. Russia controlled a colony there from 1812 to 1841. During this time, it also

As more settlers began to travel to Oregon Country, the U.S. government grew increasingly concerned about the control other nations, including Russia, had in that area.

Shown here is an image of a 19th-century Russian settlement in present-day Alaska.

claimed land in Oregon Country, which was located in what's now the Pacific Northwest region of the United States.

Monroe worried about the growing influence of Russia in addition to the other European nations that controlled lands in what's now the western United States. These other European nations included Spain and Britain. In fact, historians believe Monroe's concerns over Russian territory spreading from Alaska to California helped lead to the creation of the Monroe Doctrine.

FREEDOM COMES TO LATIN AMERICA

Although concern over Russia expanding its territory in North America was a factor in the creation of the Monroe Doctrine, the biggest factor was the fear of European influence returning to **Latin America**. After the **Napoleonic Wars** ended in 1815, Spain's empire in the Western Hemisphere fell apart. Between 1815 and the creation of the Monroe Doctrine, several Latin

Shown here is an image of a battle during Peru's fight for independence from Spain.

This painting shows a battle during the Napoleonic Wars. After these wars, Spain lost control over many of its colonies in the Western Hemisphere.

American nations declared their independence from Spain, including what's now Argentina, Peru, and Mexico.

U.S. leaders didn't want European nations to join together to turn those independent countries back into colonies. They were especially afraid of Spain and France seeking to regain control of areas they once governed. One way those nations could do this was by putting a puppet monarch in charge of a country. A puppet monarch is a leader who appears to be an independent ruler but was placed on the throne by a colonial power that still controls the decisions made in that country.

ASKING FOR ADVICE

The threat of France and Spain joining together to take back their former colonies in the Western Hemisphere worried British leaders, too. George Canning, who was the British foreign minister, suggested to Monroe that their two countries work together to speak out against any further colonization in the Western Hemisphere.

Monroe reached out to former presidents Thomas Jefferson and James Madison for foreign policy advice. Both men told Monroe

George Canning

This painting, which is meant to represent the creation of the Monroe Doctrine, can be found in the U.S. Capitol in Washington, D.C.

that the best course of action was to form an alliance with Britain. However, John Quincy Adams didn't agree with Jefferson and Madison. He believed it would be best for the United States to stand on its own and issue its own statement against future colonization in its hemisphere.

Ultimately, Monroe decided to listen to Adams. On December 2, 1823, Monroe delivered his yearly address to Congress. In it, he expressed what has become known as the Monroe Doctrine.

FROM POWERLESS TO POWERFUL

The Monroe Doctrine's four basic points were very clear. First, the United States wouldn't interfere in European affairs. Second, it wouldn't interfere with existing colonies in the Western Hemisphere. Third, the Western Hemisphere was closed to further colonization. Finally, any act to create a new colony or interfere with an existing nation in the Western Hemisphere would be seen as a hostile act against the United States.

While these points seemed like important foreign policy foundations, they were largely ignored in Europe. The United States didn't have the military power to enforce these policies in 1823. This made it hard for European leaders to take what Monroe had said seriously.

However, as the United States began to expand throughout the 19th century, the young nation became more powerful. It began to rely on the points made in the Monroe Doctrine as its influence started to extend beyond its borders and into other parts of the Western Hemisphere.

As the United States expanded westward into areas such as present-day Nevada, shown here in 1875, it became a more powerful force in the Western Hemisphere. By the mid-1800s, it was able to back up the words of the Monroe Doctrine with actions.

A SEPARATE SPHERE OF INFLUENCE

The Monroe Doctrine drew a clear line between the "New World" of the Western Hemisphere and the "Old World" of Europe. In doing so, it established a sphere of influence in the Americas that was separate from any European sphere of influence. A sphere of influence is an area of the world in which one country has unofficial power over other countries in that area. Those countries can still have their own leaders. However, one country—through

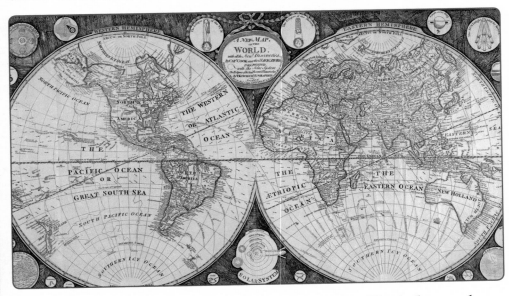

This map shows the separation between the Western Hemisphere and the Eastern Hemisphere.

*Political cartoons were sometimes used to show the influence of the United States over its Latin American neighbors. In this political cartoon, the United States is shown as a big rooster, standing between the Latin American birds and the European birds kept in a **coop** by the Monroe Doctrine.*

economic, political, or military strength—has some level of control over what happens within its sphere.

The Monroe Doctrine positioned the United States at the center of its own sphere of influence. It did this by forbidding future attempts at colonization in the Western Hemisphere. As the 19th century went on, the influence of the United States on affairs throughout the Western Hemisphere only grew stronger.

ENFORCING THE MONROE DOCTRINE

President James K. Polk **reaffirmed** the central ideas of the Monroe Doctrine during his first annual address to Congress in 1845. In his address, he stated that the Monroe Doctrine would be applied with "greatly increased force" if Europeans tried to colonize "any part of the North American continent." He was especially concerned with Britain's presence in Oregon Country. This concern led to the establishment of a set border between the United States and Britain in Oregon Country in 1846.

The Monroe Doctrine was also **invoked** when the United States sent troops to the Rio Grande in 1865. Its goal was to support the overthrow of Emperor Maximilian, who was the puppet monarch France put on the Mexican throne.

In 1867, Mexican President Benito Juárez's campaign against France's puppet monarchy ended successfully. The United States helped remove a European power from North America, putting the Monroe Doctrine into action in a way Europe could no longer ignore.

While the **American Civil War** was occupying the attention of U.S. leaders, France took control of Mexico and placed Maximilian, shown here, on the throne. Once the American Civil War ended in 1865, the United States turned its attention to enforcing the Monroe Doctrine and ending France's puppet monarchy in Mexico.

THE ROOSEVELT COROLLARY

A new era in American foreign policy began with the 20th century. In 1902, several European governments took action against Venezuela when that country couldn't pay its **debts**. President Theodore Roosevelt worried that this event could lead to increased European interference in the Western Hemisphere.

Roosevelt wanted to do what he could to protect America's standing as a growing world power. In

President Theodore Roosevelt is shown pointing to Latin America on a globe in this painting.

The Roosevelt Corollary to the Monroe Doctrine was seen as part of Roosevelt's "Big Stick" approach to foreign policy in Latin America. That term came from a phrase Roosevelt liked to use: "Speak softly and carry a big stick."

December 1904, he addressed Congress and presented what became known as the Roosevelt Corollary to the Monroe Doctrine. A corollary is something that naturally follows from something else. This corollary stated that the Monroe Doctrine justified the use of force to respond to problems in Latin America.

The Roosevelt Corollary to the Monroe Doctrine put the United States in the position of an international police power. It was used to justify U.S. actions in a number of Latin American countries in the early 1900s, including Cuba, Nicaragua, and Haiti.

A UNIQUELY AMERICAN FOREIGN POLICY

The Monroe Doctrine was invoked at other times during the 20th century, too. In 1962, the Soviet Union was building sites in Cuba from which to launch **missiles**. This action went against the Monroe Doctrine and threatened U.S. national security, so the U.S. government took action with a **blockade**. After a standoff that lasted days, the Soviet Union pulled its missiles out of Cuba. During the Cuban Missile Crisis, the United States was supported by the Organization of American States (OAS). The OAS was formed in 1948 to bring together the nations of the Americas to work with each other and defend each other's independence.

The United States has grown into a powerful and influential nation—not just in the Western Hemisphere, but around the world. That all began almost 200 years ago with the Monroe Doctrine. With one address from President James Monroe, a uniquely American foreign policy was born, and global politics changed forever.

GLOSSARY

American Civil War (uh-MEHR-uh-kuhn SIH-vuhl WOR): A war fought from 1861 to 1865 between the North and the South in the United States over slavery and other issues.

blockade (blah-KAYD): The action of cutting off an area with troops or warships to stop the entrance or exit of people or supplies.

coop (KOOP): A cage or small building for housing chickens or small animals.

debt (DEHT): Money owed to another.

invoke (ihn-VOHK): To appeal to something as an authority for an action.

Latin America (LAA-tuhn uh-MEHR-uh-kuh): All the Americas south of the United States.

missile (MIH-suhl): An object that is shot or launched to strike something from a distance.

Napoleonic Wars (nuh-poh-lee-AAN-ihk WORS): A series of conflicts from 1803 to 1815 between the French Empire and other European powers.

reaffirm (ree-uh-FUHRM): To state again as a fact.

secretary of state (SEHK-ruh-ter-ee UHV STAYT): The head of the State Department in the United States, who is in charge of foreign affairs.

uniquely (yoo-NEEK-lee): Being the only one of its kind.

INDEX

PRIMARY SOURCE LIST

Page 4: Portrait of James Monroe. Created by Samuel Morse. ca. 1819. Oil on canvas. Now kept at the White House, Washington, D.C.

Page 5: Text of the Monroe Doctrine. Created by James Monroe. 1823. Now kept at the National Archives, Washington, D.C.

Page 6: Portrait of John Quincy Adams. Created by Gilbert Stuart. 1818. Oil on canvas. Now kept at the White House, Washington, D.C.

Page 17: *His Foresight.* Created by John S. Pughe. 1901. Print published in *Puck* magazine. Now kept at the Library of Congress, Prints and Photographs Division, Washington, D.C.

WEBSITES

Due to the changing nature of Internet links, PowerKids Press has developed an online list of websites related to the subject of this book. This site is updated regularly. Please use this link to access the list: www.powerkidslinks.com/soah/mondoc